Reading Mastery

Signature Edition

Literature Guide
Grade K

Siegfried Engelmann

McGraw Hill **SRA**

Columbus, OH

SRAonline.com

Copyright © 2008 by SRA/McGraw-Hill.

All rights reserved. No part of this publication may be reproduced or distributed in any form or by any means, or stored in a database or retrieval system, without the prior written consent of The McGraw-Hill Companies, Inc., including, but not limited to, network storage or transmission, or broadcast for distance learning.

Printed in the United States of America.

Send all inquiries to this address:
SRA/McGraw-Hill
4400 Easton Commons
Columbus, OH 43219

ISBN: 978-0-07-612236-3
MHID: 0-07-612236-0

17 18 19 20 LOV 19 18

The **McGraw·Hill** Companies

Contents

Reading Mastery, Grade K
Literature Guide

INTRODUCTION

Ten literature selections are designed to accompany *Reading Mastery Signature Edition,* Grade K. The selections elaborate on skills children are learning in *Reading Mastery,* provide them with a wider genre of literature than provided elsewhere in the program, and sharpen their understanding of story grammar, structure, and morals developed in *Reading Mastery*.

Below is a list of the selections and an indication of the earliest *Reading Mastery* lesson after which each selection is to be presented. The first five selections have predictable text that is presented either in rhyme or in a thematic context that is familiar to the children. These five stories are designed so children can recite words from the text. Selections 6-10 are increasingly advanced.

LITERATURE SELECTIONS

Follows Lesson	Title	Author
20	*What Are You Called?*	Honey Andersen and Bill Reinholtd
35	*Dog Went for a Walk*	Sally Farrell Odgers
50	*Goodnight*	Penelope Coad
65	*Farmer Schnuck*	Brenda Parkes
80	*This and That*	Vic Warren
95	*Henrietta's First Winter*	Rob Lewis
110	*Maxie's Cat*	Carol Carrick
125	*The Perfects*	Marjorie Weinman Sharmat
140	*Nibbly Mouse*	David Drew
155	*Little Dinosaur*	Trevor Wilson

Story Summaries

What Are You Called? presents information about names of baby animals (pup, foal, calf, cub, kid). The text follows a repetitive format: "A baby _____ is called a _____, but so is a baby . . ." (Children indicate the other animal that has the same baby name.)

Dog Went for a Walk has a repetitive text that relates who walked the dog and what the dog did. (Dog went for a walk with Jenny. Dog got hungry.) The structure of the story permits interesting rereading of the text. Children indicate what the dog will do after each walk. They also answer questions about the person associated with each outcome. (Who did Dog walk with just before he got sleepy?)

Goodnight is a predictable text that has rhyming words. (This little fish sleeps in the sea. This little bird sleeps in the tree.) The structure permits engagement of children when the story is reread. (This little fish sleeps in . . . This little bird sleeps in . . .)

Farmer Schnuck uses a format of repeated expressions to introduce new characters. Rereading of this story permits children to complete expressions and indicate what will happen next in the story.

This and That introduces different compound words and shows pictures of the component words. (Take some **butter.** Add a **fly.** Now you have a . . . **butterfly.**) Like the other books in the first set, *This and That* promotes participation of children when they put the component words together and take the compound words apart. (What words did you put together to make **butterfly?**). Also like the other stories in the first set, *This and That* works on skills that are important for the beginning reader.

Henrietta's First Winter is a story with a traditional story grammar. Henrietta has the task of gathering food for the winter. She encounters a series of problems in repeated attempts to fill her cupboard. The illustrations provide details that enrich the text.

Maxie's Cat is the story of a cat who warns two friends about a fire in the house. The story presents interesting details about cats and lends itself to questions about their behavior and other details of the plot.

The Perfects is a humorous story about a family that is perfect and their goal of finding a perfect spot for the perfect picnic. The story carries several possible morals: There's more than one way to view perfection (perfect disaster); if one searches for perfection, one may pass up important opportunities.

Nibbly Mouse is about a mouse that eats holes in the pages of the book. The holes reveal parts of pictures, while the text gives sound clues about the objects. For example, "Nibbly Mouse ate a hole in my apple. Then what did she see? It starts with *b*." Through the hole we see a pattern, but we don't know until we turn the page that the object is a blanket. Although this story is not as sophisticated as some of the others in the second set of five stories, it could not be presented earlier because children are not introduced to the sound symbol **b** in *Reading Mastery* until lesson 140.

Little Dinosaur is frustrated because he is so small compared to the brontosaurus, pteranodon, and diplodocus. In the end, he discovers that he is very large compared to a teeny, weeny dinosaur. The story presents possible morals: Size is relative; the way people feel about themselves has a lot to do with how others respond to them.

Presenting the Books

Setup. Ideally, the books should *not* be presented as part of the regular reading lessons, but during a time when children do extensions or independent work, or before or after the reading lesson. Scheduling the literature lesson at a time that is removed from the reading period is preferable.

Books may be presented to the entire class; however, it may be difficult for all children to see the illustrations if you present from the front of the room.

A workable plan is to present to the entire class, but to arrange a schedule for circulating the books to the children. You may want to make books that have been read available to the children after they complete their seatwork for particular subjects.

For lower-level performers, it is preferable to present the stories in a small group so you can make sure that the children are responding to the questions and are understanding both text and illustrations.

SCHEDULE OF LITERATURE SELECTIONS

Reading Mastery Lesson	5	10	15	20	25	30	35	40	45	50	55	60	65	70	75	80
Title																
What Are You Called?				•	•	•										
Dog Went for a Walk							•	•	•							
Goodnight										•	•	•				
Farmer Schnuck													•	•	•	
This and That																•
Henrietta's First Winter																
Maxie's Cat																
The Perfects																
Nibbly Mouse																
Little Dinosaur																

Schedule. Each book should be read to the children at least three times. Repetition assures that the children will learn the sequence and story grammar of each selection. As a general rule, present the first reading of the story as soon as the children complete the specified lesson indicated for the story introduction. For instance, as soon as the children complete *Reading Mastery* lesson 20, present *What Are You Called?*

Schedule the second reading of the story about five lessons later and the third reading of the story about ten lessons later. Here's a possible schedule that shows three readings for each book. This schedule provides for literature selections every fifth lesson (or every fifth day.)

Reading selections to the children. Presentation questions for each selection are provided in this guide.

For some of the selections, the questions are different for the first and second presentations. Note that the questions do not cover everything you might feel the children should respond to, but focus

Reading Mastery Lesson	85	90	95	100	105	110	115	120	125	130	135	140	145	150	155	160	165
Title																	
What Are You Called?																	
Dog Went for a Walk																	
Goodnight																	
Farmer Schnuck																	
This and That	•	•															
Henrietta's First Winter				•	•	•											
Maxie's Cat						•	•	•									
The Perfects									•	•	•						
Nibbly Mouse												•	•	•			
Little Dinosaur															•	•	•

more on the reading-related skills that will help them as they progress through *Reading Mastery*. As a general rule, children should understand the pictures and should have time to study the pictures and text, and they should hear the selection frequently enough for the details and the sequence to become familiar.

Following the introduction of each selection, arrange times when the children can study the selection, either individually or as partners. Some of them may be able to read the words or may ask about the words. Do not require them to meet specific reading standards, but give them positive reinforcement for observing the written words and applying what they have learned to those words that they can decode. For top readers, you may do a kind of read-along, in which children point to the words as you read them.

Above all, try to keep the story time a reinforcing activity. Maintain focus on the story and the content. Keep the morals or lessons learned from the stories brief. Model enjoyment of the stories, and generally treat story time as just that—a treat.

What Are You Called?

Written by Honey Andersen and Bill Reinholtd
Illustrated by Julian Bruere

What Are You Called? presents information about names of baby animals (pup, foal, calf, cub, kid). The text follows a repetitive format: "a baby _____ is called a _____, but so is a baby . . ." (Children indicate the other animal that has the same baby name.)

	Follows *Reading Mastery* Lesson
First Reading	20
Second Reading	25
Third Reading	30

First Reading

Page 3
- *(Show picture.) What kind of animal is on this page? Dog.*

    A baby dog is called a pup, but so is a baby . . .

Page 4
- (Show picture.) What kind of animal is on this page? *Seal.* Yes, a baby seal is called a pup.
- Listen:

    A baby dog is called a pup, but so is a baby . . . *Seal.*

Page 5
- (Show picture.) What kind of animal is on this page? *Cow.*

    A baby cow is called a calf, but so is a baby . . .

Page 6
- (Show picture.) What kind of animal is on this page? *Elephant.* Yes, a baby elephant is called a calf.
- Listen:

    A baby cow is called a calf, but so is a baby . . . *Elephant.*

Page 7
- (Show picture.) What kind of animal is on this page? *Horse.*

    A baby horse is called a foal, but so is a baby . . .

Page 8
- (Show picture.) What kind of animal is on this page? *Donkey.* Yes, a baby donkey is called a foal.
- Listen:

    A baby horse is called a foal, but so is a baby . . . *Donkey.*

Page 9
- (Show picture.) What kind of animal is on this page? *Fox.*

  A baby fox is called a cub, but so is a baby . . .

Page 10
- (Show picture.) What kind of animal is on this page? *Tiger.* Yes, a baby tiger is called a cub.
- Listen:

  A baby fox is called a cub, but so is a baby . . . *Tiger.*

Page 11
- (Show picture.) What kind of animal is on this page? *Goat.*

  A baby goat is called a kid, and sometimes . . .

Page 12
- (Show picture.) What kind of animal is on this page? *Kids.* Yes, baby humans are called kids.
- Listen:

  A baby goat is called a kid, and sometimes . . .

  We are called kids, too.

Second Reading and Third Reading

Page 3
- (Show picture.) What kind of animal is on this page? *Baby dog; pup.* What is a baby dog called? *Pup.*

  A baby dog is called a pup, but so is a baby . . . *what? Seal.*

Page 4
- (Show picture.) What kind of animal is on this page? *Baby seal*

  A baby dog is called a pup, but so is a baby . . . *Seal.*

Page 5
- (Show picture.) What kind of animal is on this page? *Baby cow; calf.* What is a baby cow called? *Calf.*

  A baby cow is called a calf, but so is a baby . . . *what?*

  Elephant.

Page 6
- (Show picture.) What kind of animal is on this page? *Baby elephant.*

  A baby cow is called a calf, but so is a baby . . . *Elephant.*

Page 7
- (Show picture.) What kind of animal is on this page? *Baby horse; foal.* What is a baby horse called? *Foal.*

  A baby horse is called a foal, but so is a baby . . . *what?*

  Donkey.

Page 8
- (Show picture.) What kind of animal is on this page? *Baby donkey.*

  A baby horse is called a foal, but so is a baby . . . *Donkey.*

Page 9
- (Show picture.) What kind of animal is on this page? *Baby fox; cub.* What is a baby fox called? *Cub.*

  A baby fox is called a cub, but so is a baby . . . *what? Tiger.*

Page 10   • (Show picture.) What kind of animal is on this page?
                   Baby tiger.

                     A baby fox is called a cub, but so is a baby . . . *Tiger.*

Page 11   • (Show picture.) What kind of animal is on this page?
                   Baby goat; kid. What is a baby goat called? *Kid.*

                     A baby goat is called a kid, and sometimes . . . *what?*
                   We are called kids, too.

Page 12   • (Show picture.) What kind of animal is on this page?
                   Kids; *children.*

                     A baby goat is called a kid, and sometimes . . .
                   We are called kids, too.

Dog Went for a Walk

Written by Sally Farrell Odgers
Illustrated by Peter Shaw

Dog Went for a Walk has repetitive text that relates who walked the dog and what the dog did. (Dog went for a walk with Jenny. Dog got hungry.) The structure of the story permits interesting rereading of the text. Children indicate what the dog will do after each walk. They also answer questions about the person associated with each outcome.

	Follows *Reading Mastery* Lesson
First Reading	35
Second Reading	40
Third Reading	45

First Reading

Page 3
- (Show picture.)
  Dog went for a walk with Jenny.
  Is Jenny having an easy time with Dog? *No.*

Page 4
- (Show picture.)
  Dog got hungry.
  What happened to Dog when Dog went for a walk with Jenny? *Dog got hungry.*
  What's Dog eating? *A bone.*

Page 5
- (Show picture.)
  Dog went for a walk with Tom.
  Is Tom having an easy time with Dog? *No.*

Page 6
- (Show picture.)
  Dog got sleepy.
  What happened after Dog went for a walk with Tom? *Dog got sleepy.*

Page 7
- (Show picture.)
  Dog went for a walk with David.
  Is David having an easy time with Dog? *No.*
  What's Dog after in that picture? *Ducks.*

Page 8   • (Show picture.)
             Dog got wet.
             What happened after Dog went for a walk with David? *Dog got wet.*

Page 9   • (Show picture.)
             Dog went for a walk with Mom.
             Is Mom having an easy time with Dog? *No.*

Page 10   • (Show picture.)
             Dog got dirty.
             What happened after Dog went for a walk with Mom? *Dog got dirty.*

Page 11   • (Show picture.)
             Dog went for a walk with Dad.
             Is Dad having an easy time? *No.*
             Why does Dog look so dirty and wet? *It's muddy; it's been raining.*

Page 12   • (Show picture.)
             Dog got a bath.
             What happened after Dog went for a walk with Dad? *Dog got a bath.*

Second Reading

This time, see if you remember what happened to Dog after each walk.

Page 3   • (Show picture.)
             Dog went for a walk with Jenny.
             Who remembers what happened to Dog after this walk? *Dog got hungry.*
             (Show picture on page 4.)
             Dog got hungry.

Page 5   • (Show picture.)
             Dog went for a walk with Tom.
             Who remembers what happened to Dog after this walk? *Dog got sleepy.*
             (Show picture on page 6.)
             Dog got sleepy.

Page 7   • (Show picture.)
             Dog went for a walk with David.
             Who remembers what happened to Dog after this walk? *Dog got wet.*
             (Show picture on page 8.)
             Dog got wet.

Page 9   • (Show picture.)
             Dog went for a walk with Mom.
             Who remembers what happened to Dog after this walk? *Dog got dirty.*
             (Show picture on page 10.)
             Dog got dirty.

Page 11   • (Show picture.)
                     Dog went for a walk with Dad.
                 Who remembers what happened to Dog after this walk? *Dog got a bath.*
                 (Show picture on page 12.)
                     Dog got a bath.
                 Who thinks that Dog really needed a bath?

Third Reading

(Follow instructions for **Second Reading.** In addition, ask questions about the person associated with each outcome.) Who did Dog walk with just before he got sleepy?

Goodnight

Written by Penelope Coad
Illustrated by Dominique Falla

Goodnight is a predictable text that has rhyming words. (This little fish sleeps in the sea. This little bird sleeps in the tree.) The structure permits engagement of children when the story is reread. (This little fish sleeps in . . . This little bird sleeps in . . .)

	Follows *Reading Mastery* Lesson
First Reading	50
Second Reading	55
Third Reading	60

All Readings

Page 3
- (Show picture.)
  This little fish sleeps in the sea.
  Where does it sleep? *In the sea.*

Page 4
- (Show picture.)
  This little bird sleeps in the tree.
  Where does the little bird sleep? *In the tree.*
- Listen to the first part again and tell me the missing words.
  This little fish sleeps in the sea.
  This little bird sleeps . . . *In the tree.*

Page 5
- (Show picture.)
  This little horse sleeps on his legs.
  What does this little horse sleep on? *His legs.*

Page 6
- (Show picture.)
  This little hen sleeps on her eggs.
  What does this little hen sleep on? *Her eggs.*
- Listen to that part again and tell me the missing words.
  This little horse sleeps on his legs.
  This little hen sleeps . . . *On her eggs.*

Page 7
- (Show picture.)
  This little pig sleeps in a pen.
  Where does this little pig sleep? *In a pen.*

Page 8	• (Show picture.)
	   This little fox sleeps in a den.
	Where does this little fox sleep? *In a den.*
	• Listen to that part again and tell me the missing words.
	   This little pig sleeps in a pen.
	   This little fox sleeps . . . *In a den.*

Page 9	• (Show picture.) This little lamb sleeps by the door. Where does this little lamb sleep? *By the door.*

Page 10	• (Show picture.)
	   This little dog sleeps on the floor.
	Where does this little dog sleep? *On the floor.*
	• Listen to that part again and tell me the missing words.
	   This little lamb sleeps by the door.
	   This little dog sleeps . . . *On the floor.*

Page 11	• (Show picture. Point to joey.) This is a baby kangaroo. It is called a joey. This little joey sleeps in a pouch. Where does this little joey sleep? *In a pouch.*

Page 12	• (Show picture.)
	   This little cat sleeps on the couch.
	Where does this little cat sleep? *On the couch.*
	• Listen to that part again and tell me the missing words.
	   This little joey sleeps in a pouch.
	   This little cat sleeps . . . *On the couch.*

Page 13	• (Show picture.) This little bat sleeps overhead. Where does this little bat sleep? *Overhead.*

Pages 14–15	• (Show picture.) And me? I sleep . . . in my bed.
	• Listen to that part again and tell me the missing words.
	   This little bat sleeps overhead.
	   And me? I sleep . . . *In my bed.*

Page 16	• (Show picture.) Good night.

Farmer Schnuck

Written by Brenda Parkes
Illustrated by Philip Webb

Farmer Schnuck uses a format of repeated expressions to introduce new characters. Rereading of this story permits children to complete expressions and indicate what will happen next in the story.

	Follows *Reading Mastery* Lesson
First Reading	65
Second Reading	70
Third Reading	75

First Reading Only

First I'll read the story to you. Then we'll see if you remember some of the missing words. (Show pictures and read text.)

All Readings

Let's read that book again.

Page 2
- (Show picture.)
  One Monday morning, Farmer Schnuck bought a shiny, new red truck.
  "Let's take a ride," said Mrs. Schnuck.
  "Let's take a ride in our new red truck."

Page 3
- (Show picture.)
  "Quack, quack," said the . . . *Duck.*
  "Can I come, too?"
  And Farmer Schnuck said,
  "Yes, . . ." *Please do.*
  So in waddled Duck.

Page 4
- (Show picture.)
  "Oink, oink," said the . . . *Pig.*
  "Can I? . . ." *Come, too?*
  And Farmer Schnuck said,
  "Yes, . . ." *Please do.*
  So in trotted Pig.

Page 5	• (Show picture.)
	"Woof, woof," said the . . . *Dog.*
	"Can I? . . . " *Come, too?*
	And Farmer Schnuck said . . .
	Yes, please do.
	So in jumped Dog.

Page 6	• (Show picture.)
	"Moo, moo," said the . . . *Cow.*
	"Can I? . . . " *Come, too?*
	And Farmer Schnuck said . . .
	Yes, please do.
	So in walked Cow.

Page 7	• (Show picture.)
	"Away we go," cried Mrs. . . . *Schnuck.*
	"Away we go in our new red . . ." *Truck.*

Page 8	• (Show picture.)
	Through the gate.

Page 9	• (Show picture.)
	and past the mill,

Page 10	• (Show picture.)
	over the bridge,

Page 11	• (Show picture.)
	and up the . . . *Hill.*

Page 12	• (Show picture.)
	faster and **faster** and **FASTER**
	until . . .

Page 13	• (Show picture.)
	BUMP!

Page 14	• (Show picture.)
	The truck stopped still.

Page 15	• (Show picture.)
	"Get back in," cried the Schnucks.
	"Please do."
	But the animals all said . . .

Page 16	• (Show picture.) *No, thank you!*

This and That

Written by Vic Warren
Illustrated by Olivia Cole

This and That introduces different compound words and shows pictures of the component words (Take some **butter.** Add a **fly.** Now you have a . . . **butterfly.**) Like the other books in the first set, *This and That* promotes participation of children when they put the component words together and take the compound words apart (What words did you put together to get **butterfly?**). Also like the others in the first set, *This and That* works on skills that are important for the beginning reader.

	Follows *Reading Mastery* Lesson
First Reading	80
Second Reading	85
Third Reading	90

First Reading Only

I'll read the whole story and show you the pictures. Then I'll ask you questions.

Page 2	• (Show picture.)
	I bet you know all about adding numbers. But what do you know about adding words?

Page 3
• (Show picture.)
Take some **butter.**
Add a **fly.**
Now you have a . . .

Page 4
• (Show picture.)
butterfly.

Page 5
• (Show picture.)
Put a **foot**
with a **ball.**
Now you have a . . .

Page 6
• (Show picture.)
football.

Page 7	• (Show picture.)
	Take a **pan**
	and a **cake.**
	Now you have a . . .

| Page 8 | • (Show picture.) |
| | **pancake.** |

Page 9	• (Show picture.)
	When there is **rain,**
	add a **bow.**
	Now you have a . . .

| Page 10 | • (Show picture.) |
| | **rainbow.** |

Page 11	• (Show picture.)
	Add a **cup**
	and a **board.**
	Now you have a . . .

| Page 12 | • (Show picture.) |
| | **cupboard.** |

Page 13	• (Show picture.)
	Put a **star**
	with a **fish.**
	Now you have a . . .

| Page 14 | • (Show picture.) |
| | **starfish.** |

Page 15	• (Show picture.)
	Take a **book.**
	Find the **end.**
	Now you have a . . .

| Page 16 | • (Show picture.) |
| | **bookend.** |

All Readings

Now we'll read that book again.

Page 3	• (Show picture.)
	Take some **butter.** Add a **fly.** Now you have a . . . *Butterfly.*
	• What's on that butter? *A fly.*
	What funny word could you get by adding **butter** and **fly?**
	Butterfly.

| Page 4 | • (Show picture.) What is that? *Butterfly.* |

Page 5	• (Show picture.)
	Put a **foot** with a **ball.** Now you have a . . . *Football.*
	• What is that foot touching? *A ball.*
	What funny word could you get by adding **foot** and **ball?** *Football.*

Page 6	• (Show picture.) What is that? *Football.*

Page 7	• (Show picture.)
	Take a **pan** and a **cake.** Now you have a . . . *Pancake.*
	• What is the pan touching? *A cake.*
	What funny word could you get by adding **pan** and **cake?** *Pancake.*

Page 8	• (Show picture.) What is that? *Pancake.*

Page 9	• (Show picture.)
	When there is **rain,** add a **bow.** Now you have a . . . *Rainbow.*
	• What is that in her hair? *A bow.*
	Is the rain touching that bow? *Yes.*
	What funny word could you get by adding **rain** and **bow?** *Rainbow.*

Page 10	• (Show picture.) What is that? *Rainbow.*

Page 11	• (Show picture.)
	Add a **cup** and a **board.** Now you have a . . . *Cupboard.*
	• What is the cup touching? *A board.*
	What funny word could you get by adding **cup** and **board?** *Cupboard.*

Page 12	• (Show picture.) What is that? *Cupboard.*

Page 13	• (Show picture.)
	Put a **star** with a **fish.** Now you have a . . . *Starfish.*
	• What is in front of that fish? *A star.*
	What funny word could you get by adding a **star** and a **fish?** *Starfish.*

Page 14	• (Show picture.) What is that? *Starfish.*

Page 15	• (Show picture.)
	Take a **book.** Find the **end.** Now you have a . . . *Bookend.*
	• The words in the book say "The end." What do they say? *The end.*
	What funny word could you get by adding **book** and **end?** *Bookend.*

Page 16	• (Show picture.) What is that? *Bookend.*

Third Reading

(Ask Children to take the compound words apart.) What words did you put together to make butterfly?

Henrietta's First Winter

Written and Illustrated by Rob Lewis

Henrietta's First Winter is a story with a traditional story grammar. Henrietta has the task of gathering food for the winter. She encounters a series of problems in repeated attempts to fill her cupboard. The illustrations provide details that enrich the text.

	Follows *Reading Mastery* Lesson
First Reading	95
Second Reading	100
Third Reading	105

First Reading

Pages 2 and 3
- (Show pages 2–3.)
  You can see Henrietta. What color is Henrietta? *Brown.*
  What kind of animal do you think Henrietta is? *Field mouse; vole; ground squirrel.* Yes, I think she's a _____.
  What colors are the leaves? *Orange, yellow, and brown.*
  This picture shows the leaves in the fall. Fall is sometimes called *autumn.*
  What's another word for fall? *Autumn.*
    Henrietta was very young. Her mother died in the spring, just after Henrietta was born. She looked out at the autumn leaves. She had never seen leaves turn yellow and brown before.
- When did Henrietta's mother die? *In the spring; just after Henrietta was born.*
  What colors were the leaves turning now? *Yellow and brown.*
  Had Henrietta ever seen leaves do that before? *No.*

Pages 4 and 5
- (Show pages 4–5.)
  What kind of gray animals do you see in the picture? *Gray squirrels.*
    Other animals were busy collecting nuts and berries. "Henrietta, you must store up food for the winter," they said. "In the winter the trees will be bare, and there will be nothing to eat."
- What did the other animals tell her to collect? *Food for the winter.*
  If she didn't store up food, what would she have to eat during the winter? *Nothing.*
  Why wouldn't she have any food? *The trees will be bare.*

Pages 6 and 7	• (Show pages 6–7.) So Henrietta dug herself a cupboard and went out collecting nuts and berries to fill it. What did she dig in the first picture? *A cupboard.* What is that she is collecting in the second picture? *Berries.*
Pages 8 and 9	• (Show pages 8–9.) The cupboard was soon full. Henrietta sat back in her chair and fell asleep. Did it take her very long to fill the cupboard? *No.* What did she do after the cupboard was full? *Sat in her chair and fell asleep.* Look at the things in the picture. What is that thing in her fireplace? *A paper clip.* What is that thing she uses for a clock? *Part of a wristwatch.* What is her chair? *A crushed soda can.* What other tiny things do you see in that picture? *Children respond.*
Pages 10 and 11	• (Show pages 10–11.) She was awakened by a splish, splash, splish, splash. It was raining outside, but the sound was coming from inside, too. What sounds woke her up? *Splish, splash, splish, splash.* Look at the picture. Does she look happy? *No.* What was making the sounds outside? *Rain.* She also heard sounds from the inside.
Pages 12 and 13	• (Show pages 12–13.) She opened the cupboard door. With a whoosh, all Henrietta's winter food was washed away, out the front door and down the bank. What's floating out of her cupboard in the picture? *Nuts and berries.* Why did all that water get in her cupboard? *The rain.* What happened to all her winter food? *It was washed away.*
Pages 14 and 15	• (Show pages 14–15.) She mended the hole where the rain came in, put on her boots, and went out to collect more nuts and berries. She mended the hole. That means she fixed it so it wouldn't leak. Then what did she go out to collect? *More nuts and berries.* What is she carrying in the picture? *A brown nut and a red berry.*
Page 16	• (Show page 16.) At last the cupboard was full again. Henrietta made herself a hot drink, sat by the fire, and closed her sleepy eyes. What did she do just after she filled the cupboard? *Made herself a hot drink.* How did she feel? *Sleepy.* What is she heating in the picture? *A drink.*

Page 17	• (Show page 17.)
	She woke up suddenly. There was a munching sound coming from the cupboard. Henrietta opened the door.

Page 18	• (Show page 18.)
	The cupboard was full of creepy, crawly creatures eating her acorns, nuts, and berries. "Yum, yum! Very nice!" they said.
	What was making the noise in her cupboard? *Creepy, crawly creatures.*
	Look at the picture. What are those creepy, crawly creatures doing? *Eating.*

Page 19	• (Show page 19.)
	She chased them outside. Poor Henrietta. All she had left was a pile of nutshells. Tomorrow she would have to go out and collect some more.
	What did she do with the creepy, crawly creatures? *Chased them outside.*
	What was left of her winter food? *A pile of nutshells.*
	What would she have to do tomorrow? *Go out and collect some more.*

Pages 20 and 21	• (Show pages 20–21.)
	The next day, the weather was cold and damp. Nearly all the leaves had fallen from the trees, and there weren't many nuts and berries left. It would take Henrietta a long time to collect enough to fill her cupboard, and she was very tired.
	Was the weather getting better or worse? *Worse.*
	Were there a lot of nuts and berries around for her to gather? *No.*
	Was she able to pick them up quickly? *No.*
	How did she feel as she worked? *Very tired.*
	She wants to sleep, doesn't she? *Yes.*
	Look at the picture. Are there a lot of leaves left on the trees? *No.*

Pages 22 and 23	• (Show pages 22–23.)
	The other animals were watching Henrietta. Out of their nests and holes they came. They all helped to fill her cupboard again.
	What did the other animals help Henrietta do? *Fill her cupboard again.*
	Look at the picture. What kinds of animals do you see in that picture? *Gray squirrels, hedgehog, field mice (or voles).*

Page 24	• (Show page 24.)
	Henrietta was so pleased that she had a tea party. It was a great success.
	What kind of party did she have? *A tea party.*
	Look at the picture. Who is at her party? *Birds, squirrels, mole, hedgehog, field mice (and/or voles).*

Page 25	• (Show page 25.)

But when everyone had gone home, Henrietta found they had eaten all her food.

How much food was left at the end of the party? *None.*

Who ate it all? *They did; everyone at the party.*

Look at the picture. What is Henrietta looking at? *Her bare cupboard.*

Pages 26 and 27	• (Show pages 26–27.)

She looked out her window. Snow was falling. What could she do? There were no more nuts and berries left.

What was happening outside? *Snow was falling.*

How much will she have to eat? *Nothing.*

Look at the picture. How cold does it look in that picture? *Very cold.*

Soon, everything will be covered with snow. Were there any nuts and berries out there? *No.*

Pages 28 and 29	• (Show pages 28–29.)

She was very tired and very full of party food. "I'll have just a little sleep," she said to herself. "Then I'll see if I can find a few scraps of food under the snow." When she woke up . . .

What did she decide to do right away? *Have a little sleep.*

What did she plan to do after she woke up? *Find a few scraps of food under the snow.*

Look at the picture. What is she using for a bed? *A sardine can.*

Yes.

When she woke up . . .

Page 30	• (Show page 30.)

it was spring!

She slept all winter. Some animals do that. It's called *hibernating.*

LITERATURE LESSON 7
Maxie's Cat

Written by Carol Carrick
Illustrated by Kersti Frigell

Maxie's Cat is the story of a cat who warns two friends about a fire in the house. The story presents interesting details about cats and lends itself to questions about their behavior and other details of the plot.

	Follows *Reading Mastery* Lesson
First Reading	110
Second Reading	115
Third Reading	120

First Reading

Page 2

- (Show page 2.)

  Kate rang the doorbell of Maxie's house. She was carrying a big bag. The bag was so big that she couldn't see around it. Maxie's mother answered the door. "Who's there?" she asked. "Who is behind the bag?"

  Kate put down the heavy bag. "It's me," she said. "Is Maxie home?"

  Who has the big bag? *Kate.*

  Whose house is she going to? *Maxie's.*

Page 3

- (Show page 3.)

  "Come on in," said Maxie's mother. "What have you got in that bag?"

  "My pajamas," said Kate. "And I have my slippers, my toothbrush, my hairbrush, and a sweater, in case it gets cold."

  "Goodness!" said Maxie's mother. "Are you moving in?" Kate laughed. "No," she said. "I'm sleeping over."

  What are some of the things Kate had in the bag? *Pajamas, slippers, toothbrush, hairbrush, and a sweater.*

  Why did she bring all these things to Maxie's house? *She's sleeping over.*

Page 4	• (Show page 4.)
	Maxie came in from her room down the hall.
	"Hi Kate!" she said. "Did you bring your yo-yo? I'll show you some new tricks I learned."
	Kate pulled out a big purple yo-yo. It dropped and rolled across the floor.
	Just then, a fluffy gray cat jumped off the couch. He ran after the yo-yo.
	When the yo-yo stopped, he batted it under the couch.
	What did Kate drop on the floor? *A yo-yo.*
	What do you do with a yo-yo? *Make it do tricks.*
	Who ran after the yo-yo? *A fluffy gray cat.*
	You can see the cat chasing the yo-yo.
Page 5	• (Show page 5.)
	"Smokey!" said Maxie. "Give us back the yo-yo."
	The two girls looked under the couch. There was Smokey with Kate's purple yo-yo.
	When Kate reached out to get it, Smokey batted her hand.
	"Ow!" said Kate. "Why did he do that?"
	"He thinks you're playing with him," said Maxie. "Watch."
	Maxie played with the yo-yo. Up and down, and, 'round the world!
	Suddenly a furry gray arm shot out and batted the shiny, round yo-yo.
	Kate laughed.
	What is the cat's name? *Smokey.*
Page 6	• (Show page 6.)
	Soon Maxie and Katie got tired of playing. The girls walked into the kitchen.
	"I'm hungry," Maxie said to her mother.
	"How soon will we eat?"
	"Supper is almost ready," her mother said. "Why don't you girls come and help." Kate poured milk while Maxie set the table.
	"Meow," said Smokey. He was looking up at Kate. "MEOW!"
	"What does he want?" Kate asked.
	"He wants some milk," said Maxie. "It's time for him to eat, too." So she filled the cat's dish and his water bowl.
	What are the girls doing in the picture? *Helping; Kate is pouring milk, and Maxie is setting the table.*
	What does Smokey want? *Some milk.*
Page 7	• (Show page 7.)
	When supper was over, Maxie and Kate helped clear the table. Then they went down the hall to Maxie's room. Maxie had a fish tank with a bubbler and a light in it. She let Kate sprinkle food flakes on the surface of the water.
	Together, the girls watched the fish rise to the surface and eat.
	What are the girls doing in the picture? *Feeding the fish.*

Page 8	• (Show page 8.)
	They were coloring with Maxie's new crayons, when they heard a thump at the door.
	"What was that?" said Kate.
	Maxie laughed. "Smokey wants to come in."
	Sure enough, when she opened the door, Smokey walked in, his tail held high.
Page 9	• (Show page 9.)
	First he rubbed against Kate. Then he lay down on the page she was coloring. "Get off, Smokey!" said Kate. "Why are you doing that?"
	"He wants attention," said Maxie. "Here's his brush."
	Kate ran the brush over the cat's silky fur. He began to purr. "See," said Maxie. "He likes that."

What did Smokey do to get attention? *Thumped the door; rubbed against Kate; lay down on the page Kate was coloring.*
What made him purr? *Brushing his fur.*
Are the girls in the picture making that cat very happy? *Yes, he's purring.*
What are they doing? *Giving him attention; brushing and petting him.*

Page 10	• (Show page 10.)
	Before long, it was time for bed.
	The girls put on their pajamas, and Maxie let Kate use the bathroom first. Kate was in bed when Maxie came back. Smokey was curled up at the bottom of the bed. "Can Smokey stay with us?" Kate asked.
	"If he's good," said Maxie. "Sometimes he wakes up and wants to play."
	Patting Smokey's head, she turned out the light.
Page 11	• (Show page 11.)
	It took Kate a while to get to sleep. The pillow felt different from her one at home. But a comforting glow came from the fish tank. And she could feel the warm weight of Smokey by her feet. Soon she was fast asleep.

Why couldn't Kate go to sleep right away? *The pillow felt different.*

Page 12	• (Show page 12.)
	It was late at night when Kate woke. At first she didn't know where she was. Then she felt Smokey patting her cheek.
	Kate rolled over. "Go away," she said. "I don't want to play. I want to sleep."
	"Meow," said Smokey. *"MEOW!"*
	Then Kate smelled it—SMOKE! She opened her eyes. The fish tank light was on.
	What should I do? she wondered. Kate shook her friend. "Maxie! Maxie! Wake up!"

Who woke up Kate? *Smokey.*
What did she smell? *Smoke.*

Page 13

- (Show page 13.)

  Just then the smoke alarm rang. Beep! Beep!

  Maxie's mother appeared in the doorway. "Hurry, girls," she said. "Get up!"

  The two girls jumped out of bed, their eyes wide.

  "Follow me quickly out the front door. We need to go next door and call 911."

  What woke up Maxie's mother? *The smoke alarm.*

  Where did the girls go? *Next door.*

  They had to call a number. What number is that? *911; emergency.*

  Why did they need to call 911? *To report an emergency; to report the smoke.*

Page 14

- (Show page 14.)

  The girls and Maxie's mother hurried out of the house. Kate held the cat tightly.

  It seemed only minutes before the firefighters arrived. The girls and Maxie's mother waited in the front yard until the firefighters came out of the house.

  Did it take a long time for the firefighters to arrive? *No.*

  Where were the girls waiting? *In the front yard.*

  You can see the fire engine pulling up in the picture.

Page 15

- (Show page 15.)

  "Fire's out," the chief told them.

  "We had too many things in Maxie's room plugged into the extension cord," said Maxie's mother. "The cord got hot and started to burn the rug."

  The chief nodded. "Lucky thing this little fellow sounded the first alarm, before the fire got out of control."

  Who gave the first warning of the fire? *Smokey.*

  The fire was caused by too many things plugged into the extension cord. The cord got hot and what started to burn? *The rug.*

Page 16

- (Show page 16.)

  Kate was still holding the cat. She rubbed her cheek against his fur. "Thank you, Smokey," she said. "You sure have the right name."

  "Meow," said the cat.

  From that day on, he was not just Maxie's cat, but a neighborhood hero known as "Smokey, the fabulous, furry fire alarm."

  What was Smokey's new name? *Smokey, the fabulous, furry fire alarm.*

The Perfects

Written by Majorie Weinman Sharmat
Illustrated by Marc Corcoran

The Perfects is a humorous story about a family that is perfect and their goal of finding a perfect spot for the perfect picnic. The story carries several possible morals: There's more than one way to view perfection (perfect disaster); if one searches for perfection, one may pass up important opportunities.

	Follows *Reading Mastery* Lesson
First Reading	125
Second Reading	130
Third Reading	135

First Reading

I'll read the story and ask you questions about it.

Page 2
- (Show page 2.)

  Each day Mr. and Mrs. Perfect said to one another, "Our teeth are perfect. Our hair is perfect. Our clothes are perfect. Our two sons are perfect. Even our two dogs are perfect. I guess we're perfect in every way you can think of and not think of."

  Things that are perfect are just the very, very best. What are some of the things they named that were perfect? *Their teeth, hair, clothes, sons, and dogs.*

Page 3
- (Show page 3.)

  Mr. and Mrs. Perfect's sons were named Fritz and Dudley.
  Mr. and Mrs. Perfect thought the names were so perfect that they named their dogs Fritz and Dudley, too.
  What were their sons named? *Fritz and Dudley.*
  How many dogs did they have? *Two.*
  What were the dogs named? *Fritz and Dudley.*

Page 4	• (Show page 4.)

Each day, Fritz and Dudley said to one another, "Our teeth are perfect. Our hair is perfect. Our clothes are perfect. Our parents are perfect. Even our two dogs are perfect. I guess we're perfect in every way you can think of and not think of."

What are some of the things Fritz and Dudley thought were perfect? *Their teeth, hair, clothes, parents, and dogs.*

Page 5	• (Show page 5.)

Each day the Perfects' dogs barked at one another.

"That must be their way of saying they are perfect, too," said Mr. Perfect.

"Makes perfect sense to me," said Mrs. Perfect.

How did the dogs tell each other that they were perfect? *They barked at one another.*

Page 6	• (Show page 6.)

One day Fritz and Dudley said to their mother and father, "It's a perfect day. Let's have a perfect picnic."

The Perfects packed a perfect lunch. They put it in a perfect picnic basket.

Off they went, in a perfect row: Mr. and Mrs. Perfect, their sons, Fritz and Dudley, and their dogs, Fritz and Dudley.

They all walked to the woods.

Do they look pretty perfect, walking in a line like that? *Yes.*

Where were they going? *On a picnic; to the woods.*

What did they plan to do in the woods? *Have a picnic.*

Page 7	• (Show page 7.)

"We must find a perfect place to eat our perfect picnic lunch," said Mrs. Perfect. At last, they came to a bench that was under a tree near a brook.

"It doesn't look perfect to me," said Mrs. Perfect. "The bench has splinters."

"And the tree keeps dropping leaves on the bench," said Mr. Perfect.

"And the brook has a strange gurgle," said Dudley.

"Even the flies aren't right," said Fritz.

They came to a brook. That's a small stream.

Is this picnic spot perfect? *No.*

What are some of the things that the Perfects don't like about it? *The bench has splinters, the tree drops leaves, the brook has a strange gurgle, and the flies aren't right.*

Page 8	• (Show page 8.)

The Perfects kept walking . . . and walking.

At last Mrs. Perfect said, "Here is a perfect place. There is no bench. There is no tree. There is no brook. And there are no flies."

The Perfects sat down.

"Ouch!" said Dudley. "I sat on a sharp rock."

"A sharp rock?" said Mr. Perfect.

Name some things this picnic spot doesn't have. *A bench, a tree, a brook, and flies.*

Does that sound like a perfect spot? *Yes.*

Who sat on the sharp rock? *Dudley.*

Page 9	• (Show page 9.)

"Ooooh!" said Fritz. "Look at all the bees!"

"Bees!" screamed Mr. and Mrs. Perfect. "It's possible that this place is not perfect after all!"

"Let's get out of here!" said Fritz.

The Perfects grabbed their picnic basket and ran off.

Do they look perfect now? *No.*

Page 10	• (Show page 10.)

"We must keep looking for the perfect place for our perfect picnic," said Mrs. Perfect.

The Perfects looked and looked. And they walked and walked.

Then Mr. Perfect shouted, "I see it! I see it!"

"I see it, too," said Mrs. Perfect. "It's the perfect place for our perfect picnic."

"I don't see anything," said Fritz. "I don't either," said Dudley.

Who saw the perfect place for a picnic? *Mr. and Mrs. Perfect.*

Who didn't see that place? *Fritz and Dudley.*

Page 11	• (Show page 11.)

"Look up there!" said Mr. Perfect. "Look way up."

Mr. Perfect pointed to a hill.

Fritz and Dudley stretched their necks.

"That's high up, all right," said Fritz.

"Are we eating in the sky?" asked Dudley.

Page 12	• (Show page 12.)
	The Perfects started to climb. They climbed for an hour.
	They huffed and puffed.
	"If you want a perfect picnic, you have to work hard for it," said Mrs. Perfect.
	Then she said something else: "OOPS!"
	Suddenly, Mrs. Perfect started to slide backward down the hill.
	Then all the Perfects started to slide backward.
	They slid and slid.
	How long did they climb? *An hour.*
	Who slipped first? *Mrs. Perfect.*
	And then what did all the Perfects do? *Slid down the hill.*
	Do they look like they are in a perfect slide? *Children respond.*
Page 13	• (Show page 13.)
	Bump! Thump!
	"Ouch!" "Ouch!" "Ouch!" "Ouch!"
	The Perfects landed in a heap at the bottom of the hill.
	"Well, we don't quite have a perfect picnic yet," said Mrs. Perfect.
	Do they look perfect now? *No.*
Page 14	• (Show page 14.)
	She looked at her family. "Our clothes are ripped. Our hair is tangled. How could this happen to the Perfects?"
	"This picnic is awful," said Fritz.
	"It's stupid," said Dudley. "I want to go back and sit on the bench under the tree near the brook. I want to have my perfect picnic there."
	"But that place was not perfect," said Mr. and Mrs. Perfect.
Page 15	• (Show page 15.)
	"I'm hungry," said Dudley.
	"So am I," said Fritz. "A picnic is for eating. It's for stuffing yourself and getting messy and dirty and having fun. It's not for being perfect."
	"Fritz is right," said Dudley.
	Mr. Perfect looked at Mrs. Perfect. "We have two smart children," they said.
	What did Fritz think a picnic should be for? *Eating; stuffing yourself and getting messy and dirty and having fun.*
	Does that sound like more fun than being perfect? *Yes.*
Page 16	• (Show page 16.)
	Then Mr. and Mrs. Perfect and their two sons, Fritz and Dudley, and their two dogs, Fritz and Dudley, walked back to the bench that was under a tree near a brook.
	They all sat down.
	"Pass the perfect sandwiches," said Mrs. Perfect.
	The Perfect family ate and ate and ate.
	At last they were perfectly stuffed, perfectly messy, and perfectly happy.
	In what ways were they perfect? *Perfectly stuffed, messy, and happy.*

LITERATURE LESSON 9
Nibbly Mouse

Written by David Drew
Illustrated by Penny Newman

> **Note:** Pronounce the quick sounds without an *uh* at the end: **b, t, c** (k), **d.** (Not buh, tuh, cuh, duh.)

Nibbly Mouse is about a mouse that eats holes in the pages of the book. The holes reveal parts of pictures, while the text gives sound clues about the objects. For example, "Nibbly Mouse ate a hole in my apple. Then what did she see? It starts with a *b*." Through the hole we see a pattern, but we don't know until we turn the page that the object is a blanket. Although this story is not as sophisticated as some of the others in the second set, it could not be presented earlier because children are not introduced to the sound symbol **b** in *Reading Mastery* until lesson 140.

	Follows *Reading Mastery* Lesson
First Reading	140
Second Reading	145
Third Reading	150

First Reading Only

First, I'll read the whole story. Then, I'll ask you questions.
(Show pictures and read text.)

All Readings

Now I'll ask questions.

Pages 2 and 3
- (Show pages 2–3.)
  Nibbly Mouse ate a hole in my apple. Then what did she see?
  It starts with **b.**
  What does it start with? *B.*

Pages 4 and 5
- (Show pages 4–5.) What is it? *A blanket.*
  Nibbly Mouse ate a hole in my blanket. Now what can this be?
  It starts with **t.**
  What does it start with? *T.*

Pages 6 and 7	• (Show pages 6–7.) What is it? *Toast.* 　Nibbly Mouse ate a hole in my toast. Then what did she see? 　It starts with **b.** What does it start with? *B.*
Pages 8 and 9	• (Show pages 8–9.) What is it? *A basket.* 　Nibbly Mouse ate a hole in my basket. Now what can this be? 　It starts with **c.** What does it start with? *C.*
Pages 10 and 11	• (Show pages 10–11.) What is it? *Cake.* 　Nibbly Mouse ate a hole in my cake. Then what did she see? 　It starts with **d.** What does it start with? *D.*
Pages 12 and 13	• (Show pages 12–13.) What is it? *A door.* 　Nibbly Mouse ate a hole in my door. 　And then she saw . . .
Pages 14 and 15	• (Show pages 14–15.) What is it? *A cat.* 　The cat! Nibbly Mouse, don't try to eat that!
Pages 16 and 17	• (Show pages 16–17.) 　Now look! 　Nibbly Mouse ate a hole in our book! What's that sticking out of the hole in the book? *A tail.*
Back cover	• (Show back cover.) There's the rest of Nibbly Mouse.

Little Dinosaur

Written by Trevor Wilson
Illustrated by Ian Forss

Little Dinosaur is frustrated because he is so small compared to the brontosaurus, pteranodon, and diplodocus. In the end, he discovers that he is very large compared to a teeny, weeny dinosaur. The story presents possible morals: Size is relative; the way people feel about themselves has a lot to do with how others respond to them.

	Follows *Reading Mastery* Lesson
First Reading	155
Second Reading	160
Third Reading	165

First Reading

I'll read the story and ask you questions about it.

Page 2   • (Show page 2.)

Long, long ago when the world was warm and steamy, strange creatures roamed about looking for food.

One day, a young dinosaur stood by a swamp. The water shone like a big mirror, reflecting the blue sky.

And it reflected the little dinosaur standing on the bank. He didn't look a bit happy.

"Why am I so small?" he wondered, staring at his reflection.

"I want to be big, like other dinosaurs."

When did this story take place? *Long, long ago.*

Was the little dinosaur happy? *No.*

Why not? *He was small; he wanted to be big.*

What did the little dinosaur want to be? *He wanted to be big.*

Page 3	• (Show page 3.)
	So he tried to make himself bigger. He huffed and he puffed and he pushed out his sides. And he stood on his toes and he stretched his head until he was sure he was tall. But when he looked back at his picture in the water, he was no bigger at all.
	What did he try to do to make himself bigger? *He huffed and puffed and pushed out his sides; he stretched.*
	He looked at his reflection in the water. If the water is very still, it's just like looking in a mirror. Did his reflection look any bigger after he did those things? *No.*
Page 4	• (Show page 4.)
	Then he had a thought. "Well, perhaps I'm strong for my size," he said hopefully. Stomping through the mud, he hit a tree and tried to push it over. "Ow!" He hit his head, but he didn't move the tree at all.
	What's he doing in the picture? *Running at the tree.*
	Did he move the tree at all? *No.*
	So was he very strong? *No.*
Page 5	• (Show page 5.)
	Poor Little Dinosaur. He wanted so much to be big and strong. Sitting on the bank feeling sorry for himself, he began to sob.
	What did he begin to do? *He began to sob.*
	That's hard crying.
Page 6	• (Show page 6.)
	A head popped up out of the pond. Slowly, a great long neck stretched towards the bank. It was a brontosaurus.
	"Hello, Little Dinosaur. Why are you crying?"
	Who came out of the pond? *A brontosaurus.*
	That's a huge dinosaur.
	What did Brontosaurus ask the little dinosaur? *Why are you crying?*
Page 7	• (Show page 7.)
	"I'm too little. Everybody is bigger than me."
	"Hmmp," grunted Brontosaurus. "Being big isn't everything. Why, I'm so heavy I can hardly get out of the water."
	"I wouldn't mind that," sobbed Little Dinosaur. "But what made you so big?"
	Why did Brontosaurus say it wasn't always good to be big? *It could hardly get out of the water.*
Page 8	• (Show page 8.)
	"Oh, I don't know. I eat a lot and sleep quite a bit."
	"I'll try that," said Little Dinosaur. "Thank you, Brontosaurus."
	"Anything to help," grunted Brontosaurus, sinking back under the water.
	How did the brontosaurus get so big? *It eats a lot and sleeps quite a bit.*
	The little dinosaur was going to try that.

Page 9

- (Show page 9.)

  So Little Dinosaur ate and ate until he couldn't manage one more shred of moss. Then he settled down for a good nap to let his body grow.

  When he awoke, he yawned and stretched. "Yes, I do believe I'm bigger," he said hopefully. He hurried to the pond mirror.

Page 10

- (Show page 10.)

  But no matter which way he turned, he looked no bigger than before. He was so disappointed that he began to sob again.

Page 11

- (Show page 11. Point to pteranodon [tu-RAN-u-don].)

  A great pteranodon flapped through the sky and landed on a big branch with a crash that shook the whole tree.

  "Hello, Little Dinosaur. Why are you crying?"

  You can see the pteranodon in the picture. It looks like a bat, but it's much, much bigger.

  What did the pteranodon ask the little dinosaur? *Why are you crying?*

Page 12

- (Show page 12.)

  The picture shows how big Pteranodon is next to the little dinosaur.

  "I'm too little. Everybody is bigger than me."

  "Aarrk," squawked Pteranodon. "Being big isn't everything. If I were as light as you, I wouldn't have to flap my wings so hard."

  "I wouldn't mind that," said Little Dinosaur. "But what made you grow so big?"

Page 13

- (Show page 13.)

  "Oh, I don't know. I hang from branches quite a bit."

  "I'll try that," said Little Dinosaur. "Thanks."

  "Anything to help," squawked Pteranodon.

  Why did the pteranodon think he got so big? *He hangs from branches quite a bit.*

Page 14

- (Show page 14.)

  So Little Dinosaur tried hanging from a branch. It wasn't easy, and he became quite dizzy, but he hung there as long as he could.

  "Oh, dear, if this is how growing big feels, I don't know that I like it," he said, as he wobbled back to the pond.

  But he didn't look one tiny bit bigger than before. Poor Little Dinosaur sobbed louder than ever.

  Look at the picture. What's he hanging by in that picture? *His tail.*

  Did that help him get any bigger? *No.*

  And he sobbed again.

Page 15

- (Show page 15. Point to diplodocus [di-PLOD-u-cus].)

  Through the trees and ferns thumped a diplodocus.

  First came his head on the end of an extremely long neck. At the other end of his tremendous body, a tail stretched back out of sight.

  "Goodness, Little Dinosaur. Why are you crying?"

  Diplodocus looks a lot like Brontosaurus, but is a little skinnier.

  What did Diplodocus ask the little dinosaur? *Why are you crying?*

Page 16	• (Show page 16.)
	"I'm too little. Everybody is bigger than me."
	"Too little?" panted Diplodocus. "Let me tell you, being big isn't everything. Why, I'm so long that I rarely see the end of my tail."
	"I wouldn't mind that," said Little Dinosaur. "But what made you grow so big?"
Page 17	• (Show page 17.)
	"Oh, I don't know. I like the leaves from the tops of trees."
	"But I can't reach way up there."
	"Here, try this."
	Diplodocus reached up to the highest tree and pulled down a large branch.
	"Thank you, Diplodocus."
	"Anything to help," puffed Diplodocus.
	Diplodocus thought that he ate some special things that made him big.
	What was that? *Leaves from the tops of trees.*
	What did Diplodocus give to the little dinosaur? *A large branch.*
Page 18	• (Show page 18.)
	So Little Dinosaur ate the leaves, every single one. They tasted different from the ferns and mosses he usually ate, and he didn't really care for them. In fact, by the time he'd finished, he didn't feel at all well.
	"Perhaps that's just because I'm growing bigger," he hoped, as he made his way back to the pond mirror.
	But he didn't look any bigger than before. Just a bit pale in the face.
	Poor Little Dinosaur. He sobbed so hard that he cried himself to sleep.
Page 19	• (Show page 19.)
	When he awoke, he rubbed his eyes and yawned and stretched. And just in case he'd grown bigger, he peeped at himself in the water.
	"I must be the smallest dinosaur in the whole wide world," he said sadly, as he wandered off through the trees.
Page 20	• (Show page 20.)
	Then, over by a bush, something caught his eye. A mound of leaves moved. As Little Dinosaur watched, a bit of eggshell pushed out from under the leaves. Little Dinosaur stared harder.
Page 21	• (Show page 21.)
	From the broken eggshell crawled the teeniest, weeniest dinosaur he had ever seen. The teeny, weeny dinosaur yawned and stretched and looked all around. When it saw Little Dinosaur, its eyes opened wide.

Page 22   • (Show page 22.)

"WOW!" it squeaked. "What made you grow so big?"

Little Dinosaur could hardly believe his ears. A warm feeling glowed through his body.

What did the teeny, weeny dinosaur ask the little dinosaur? *What made you grow so big?*

How did that make the little dinosaur feel? *Happy; warm.*

Page 23   • (Show page 23.)

"Oh! I don't know," he said grandly, swelling out his chest. "It wasn't easy, you know. I had to work at it. If you eat the right things, you might be as big as me one day." In his delight, he pushed over a rotten tree.

The picture shows him ramming into a rotten tree. He told the teeny, weeny dinosaur to eat the right things and maybe something would happen to that dinosaur. What might happen? *He might be as big as Little Dinosaur one day.*

Page 24   • (Show page 24.)

"Oh! I will! I will!" squeaked the tiny dinosaur. "Thank you."

"Anything to help," said Little Dinosaur.

And he waddled away, feeling very satisfied indeed.

Did Little Dinosaur feel bigger after he met the teeny dinosaur? *Yes.*

Did Little Dinosaur really get any bigger? *No.*

Why did he feel so much bigger and better? *He was bigger than the teeny, weeny dinosaur.*

See if you remember the dinosaurs. Which dinosaur told him to sleep a lot? *The brontosaurus; the first dinosaur.*

Which dinosaur told him to hang from branches? *The pteranodon; the second dinosaur.*

Which dinosaur told him to eat leaves from the very top of the trees? *The diplodocus; the third dinosaur.*